Made in the USA
Monee, IL
03 March 2021

61809490R00083